IS IT WORTH IT?

IS IT WORTH IT?

JEAN CLERVIL

ISBN: 1514606739
ISBN 13: 9781514606735
Library of Congress Control Number: 2015909936
CreateSpace Independent Publishing Platform
North Charleston, South Carolina

Book Cover Photo Shot by Josh Hagwood

Ordering and Booking Information:
For details on how to order bulk copies for organizations, corporations, schools
and others email booking@mrchanginglives.com
To invite Jean to speak at your conference or event, you can also email
booking@mrchanginglives.com
For other inquiries please visit www.mrchanginglives.com

CONTENTS

To my beloved mother, Marie F. Clervil, I dedicate another piece of my life's work to you because without you…life wouldn't work.

To every soul I featured in this book, I thank you for allowing me to share your story with a world that needs to hear it.

Before reading this book, do this one exercise with me. Take a deep breath in. Take a deep breath out. One more time. Inhale. Exhale. Now I need you to thank God because that wasn't your last breath...

INTRODUCTION
WHAT IS "IT"?

*B*ecause you've picked up this book, you're probably wondering what "it" is. "It" can mean various things to various people, but the "it" that I'm referring to is your dream. To be more specific, it is the pain that comes along with chasing that dream of yours. Pain is a bold word, but to me, it encompasses all of the heartache and disappointment of attempting to accomplish a goal and falling short. To me, it encompasses feeling as if all your efforts aren't enough. It encompasses questioning every day whether what I am working toward is worth it. Nobody's the same, but we're no different. I don't know what you are currently ~~going~~ growing through, but I do know what we all have in common—and that is pain. Pain single-handedly is the most relatable topic that we can talk about because we have all suffered from something. As a young adult in my twenties and an entrepreneur at that, the pain that I and most people my age and older suffer from the most comes from two things primarily:

- The process of figuring out what we are meant to do and doing it
  o Career goals, dream job, etc.
- The relationships that we build (intimate and not intimate)
  o Love, mentorship, inner circle

There are a plethora of pains that we go through, but in my experience, those stated above have cost me the most pain, along with the hundreds of thousands of youth that I speak to every day. Throughout this book, I will be focusing primarily on the journey of discovering your purpose and/or giving you the confirmation that you're already on the right path.

"The **pain** never *left*; I just made *room* for it" is a line from a poem that I wrote describing how I've dealt with my own personal pains. When the majority of people frequently suffer from the same pain, they tend to get used to the feeling. They get numb. They get so used to it that it becomes a way of life. I once heard a story of how a dog would continue to moan on its owner's porch daily. One day, the neighbor asked the owner, "Why does your dog continue to moan? It sounds painful."

The owner replied, "It is painful, because the dog is sitting on a nail."

The neighbor then replied, "So why won't the dog move?"

The owner reluctantly scoffed and said, "Because it doesn't hurt enough."

So ask yourself this: "Is the pain that I'm experiencing from my _____ worth it?" Fill in the blank with whatever unique struggle(s) that you're ~~going~~ growing through: job, school, career, dream, and so forth. Regardless of what you are currently pursuing and whether your answer is yes, no, or I don't know, by the end of this book, you will be better equipped to understand if what you're ~~going~~ growing through is worth it or just something you no longer need to invest time in. Now, I need you to understand that I've replaced *go* with *grow* throughout the book because growth is optional. You have to make the choice to grow and reach the next level in your life. Do not struggle in vain. Ultimately, we allow ourselves to ~~go~~ grow through certain things because we want progression. We want to transition from simply desiring to live the life that we dream of to actually becoming the person who has worked diligently in achieving it. And the most important part of that are the lessons we learn during the process, which inevitably makes us more valuable. Growth is the ultimate goal in every facet.

"When you go through hell, don't stop and make a home there."

— Jean Clervil

The moment two or more people find something that they can relate to, a common bond is built. The reason that you have that song on repeat is because you can relate to the lyrics as if you've written them yourself. The reason you buy that DVD is because there's something in that movie that speaks volumes to you. And the reason I am writing this book is because I believe the pain that I've ~~gone~~ grown through is something that you can overcome as well. This book is filled with my most intimate thoughts in poetry and original quotes that spoke to me when I came across them.

I have also collected heartfelt and raw testimonies from young adults answering the question, "*Is your dream and the pain that came along with it worth it to you and why?*" Throughout this book, their most intimate thoughts will be shared with you as well in order to better motivate you on your journey of living your life's purpose. I need you to know that there are two people currently reading this sentence at this very moment: the person you are and the person you want to become. The whole goal in life is to work on ourselves to become the person we need to be, the person the world needs us to be—and that is someone of service. What we set out to accomplish won't manifest unless we work on that transition. After certain poems in this book, there are questions that you must answer. By the end of this book, you'll be able to gauge whether the pain that you're currently ~~going~~ growing through is worth it or not. Again, if it is worth it, you'll be inspired enough to keep going. If it is not, you'll be motivated enough to stop wasting your time on something that you're not passionate about.

This book is for high-school students who are currently breaking under the pressure of society, wondering whether they should go to college in the fall. This book is for college students who spend more time in financial aid than they do in class. This book is for every student who needs tools for making life decisions rather than a fifteen-minute appointment with a college adviser on what course to take for a major that he or she may not be passionate about. This book is for the college graduates who receive more calls about debt than they do career opportunities. This book is for employees who are always dissatisfied at work, taking selfies because they would like to see themselves somewhere else. This book is for managers who are tired of making someone else rich instead of themselves. This book is for entrepreneurs who have been seduced by a vision that no one else can currently see. This book is for the dreamer who is working day in and day out toward a goal but has yet to see the fruit(s) of his or her labor. This book is for *you*. There are two important dates in our lives: the day we were born and the day we figure out *why* we were born. The world *needs* you. *We need you. You* woke up this morning because your work here on this earth is not done yet. *You* were born with a gift that was meant to make you and every single spirit that you encounter happy. *You* were born with a gift that will open doors for you where there were only walls. *You* have a gift. Now, let's *unwrap* it.

A person doesn't die when he or she reaches the grave, they die when their dreams do.

— *Jean Clervil*

AN ODE TO DREAMERS

Spent my gas money on a dream; shit is real—
Because where these four wheels won't take me,
my imagination sure enough will.
Spent my lunch money on a dream because my goals are starving.
The laborers are few, but there's plenty in the harvest.
Spent my rent money on a dream
because my faith needs a place to reside.
Got to evict my fears; they're better off outside.
Spent my clothing money on a dream
because success has a nice fit.
I outgrew failure since I never decided to quit.
Spent my cell-phone money on a dream
because with success was my most important conversation.
I tried to three-way faith, but fear was on call waiting.
Spent my spouse's money on a dream
because I'm having an affair.
I'm in love with success, and failure is a burden that I can no
    longer bear.

*Are you currently willing to sacrifice the things you own to
reach your goal?*
YES | NO

For most people, their fear of loss is much greater than their desire for gain. Most individuals would work much harder to hang on to what they have than to take the necessary risks to shoot for their dreams.

— Tony Robbins

MY REASON WHY

She couldn't teach me how to fight,
but she taught me what was worth fighting for.
She couldn't teach me how to tie a tie,
but she taught me that when I'm at the end of my rope,
I should tie a knot in it and hang on.
She couldn't teach me how to change a tire,
but she taught me the importance of catering to a woman who's
    tired.
She couldn't help with my homework,
but her efforts made everything at home, work.
They say it takes a village to raise a child,
but it took the strength and love of one woman to keep me alive.

Is your reason why *big enough to stop you from quitting?*
YES | NO

My passion wakes me up in the morning, not an alarm clock, because I want to see my dreams become a reality. I wake up at 5:00 a.m. every day with the objective to be just a little closer to my goals and mitigate distractions from those who can't see my vision. It takes courage to do the things most will not do, but it becomes easier when passion is the key that drives you. Most people do not understand how much effort I put into my goals, but that is OK. The moment you do it for what others think, instead of it making you happy, you've lost your dream. I eat, sleep, and breathe my dream. However, my dreams have a direct correlation to my vision. It is one thing to make something of yourself to become successful, but the real question is, how does your dream connect to your vision and your WHY? Why do you wake up early and work long hours? What is the purpose? What is your purpose?

— Matthew J. S. Aaron Jr. (age twenty-two)

THE BIGGEST LIE

"Hey, how are you doing?"
I reply, saying, "I'm fine."
Little do they know that that's the biggest lie.
There's this mountain that I'm trying to move.
There are certain parts in my life that I'm trying to improve.
I'm in this particular space that's so fucking uncomfortable.
And with this pain, I've gotten very comfortable.
Then I realize that this space is one where no one can help me,
So that when this mountain moves,
I can only give God the glory.

Are you uncomfortable with where you're at?
YES | NO

I do think that dreams are worth it. I think that it's worth it to pursue something that makes you happy to the core, something that you're extremely passionate about. My only thing is that I'm not sure what my dream is. I know that you have to be doing something in order to figure out what that dream is, but how do you know what that "something" is that you're supposed to be doing? Everybody just keeps telling me that you have to do something, and I know that I do. I don't want to do just anything. I don't want to waste my time. It's safe to say that I'm stuck in my comfort zone because it's easy. I know that I have what it takes to push myself and follow my dreams, but I don't know why every time I stand up to go do something, I sit back down (metaphorically). I think that I don't push myself because I don't know what I want to do specifically. I just get confused at times, but I do know that where I'm at is not where I want to be. I do know that I'm not meant for the typical path of going to school, getting a job, paying debt for school…I know that that's not supposed to be my story. I believe that a lot of people are wasting their lives running that rat race. Although that may be meant for some people, a lot of people like myself don't feel that way. Doing anything that doesn't make you happy or give you a sense of purpose is a waste of your time and a waste your life. Although the fear of me wasting my time constantly lingers in my head, I know that I have a purpose to pursue. I want to help other people. I want to leave a good mark on this world, even if it's just a ripple. Your dream is worth it once you figure out exactly what you want to do.

— Leigh B. (age twenty-five)

"*The day you make up your mind, your mind makes a way.*"

— *Jean Clervil*

EVERY DAY

EV-ERY DAY,
I act on beliefs that have little or no evidence to back them up.
With no sight, I walk.
With no wings, I leap.
With no key, I knock.
With no answer, I ask.
The only things that make sense are my reasons *why*.
Everything else is "unrealistic" and typical reasoning would deny.
But you know what?
I'm going to move this mountain or climb it.
I'm going to find an opportunity or create one.
I'm going to find a way or I will make one.

Has anyone ever discouraged you from chasing your dream?
YES | NO

People who say it cannot be done
should not interrupt those who are doing it.

— Chinese Proverb

This is for the basketball player that tried out for their first basketball team, went to look at the roster for the team, but their name wasn't there. For the actor/actress that spent what felt like an eternity in the mirror reciting their lines, but their name didn't get called for a role in the play. And this is for the applicant that dresses in their best attire for an interview, thinking they passed with flying colors, but never received a call. Do you remember what that felt like? Heartache, pain, turmoil, confusion, and a myriad of other emotions are just some of the feelings you endure. I am an aspiring amateur boxer pursuing a gold medal in the 2016 Olympic Games, and right before the National Golden Gloves in 2014, I was dealt a blow that knocked me. After a few MRIs, I was diagnosed with a partial tear in my left and right shoulder, bulging disc in my lower back, and a tear in my meniscus in my right knee. I was told I should never box again. Seeing the doctor even form his lips to say each of those words created a black hole within my heart engulfing my dreams. If my dream was a volcano it exploded into a million pieces with "shattered" engraved on each and every one. At first I spent many days alone in my room with tears dripping off my face and onto my boxing gloves, which I embraced so tightly. After countless days of crying and feeling like a chunk of my identity was gone, a light bulb went off. That light bulb that went off was my passion speaking to me, letting me know that if I think of something this much and have this much love for it to just go for it. There are people who have overcome cancer and become world champions and people that loss both their legs and still make it to the Olympics, so why can't I overcome adversity and make my dreams a reality? They say the window to the soul is in your eyes and I look into the eyes of many trainers as they train fighters to achieve their dreams, visibly seeing the torment of their soul and the jealousy for the very fighter they are training, all because that fighter is living the dream they themselves wished they should have lived. I cannot allow that to be me, and every day that I wake up, every moment that I am in pain due to my injuries, I think of my dream and tell myself that it is and will be all worth it. I will have that sense of self-accomplishment knowing that whether I succeeded or not, I went for it and left nothing on the table.

—Kenyon Sessoms (age twenty-seven)

I'M SCARED

What scares me is that...
I won't write your favorite poem before I'm dead.
See, I have more thoughts than I do days,
More words than I do weeks,
More metaphors than I do months.
My poetry is parental,
Because of these words I nurture,
Your thoughts I raise,
So I write today because it's my present.
I sacrifice my time to write;
Therefore, my poetry is timeless...

Would you still do what you love to do for free?
YES | NO

Photography is my passion and my dream. I have been interested in photography since I was five years old. Here's the deal: When you find something you love and lose track of time doing it, you know you are on the right path. For me, I wanted to take pictures for magazines and newspapers. I wanted to make a name for myself. It took a lot of time and money to get the skills I needed to learn the craft. I tried for two years to get into magazines and kept getting rejected. It got to the point where I thought, "Maybe I'm not good enough." I was ready to give up. I got up the nerve to ask the editor at one of the magazines if he thought I had talent and if he had suggestions for me so I could shoot photos he would want to publish. He told me that he did think I was good enough, but I needed to make some adjustments to the way I took the photos. After I did that, I had my first two-page spread and magazine cover within six months! I am grateful for his words of encouragement to this day! Here's the deal: Following your dreams takes guts. It involves sacrifice and can include lots of rejection and failure. I have had financial hardship and major setbacks along the way, but I am still in business and doing what I love. You have to evolve. If something's not working, you have to be willing to change. Remember, every experience is pushing you in the direction you need to go. For me, I would rather do what I love and starve than do something I hate and make lots of money. We all have gifts we are given; it is our job to find out what that is and use it! We can't expect others to understand our dream, but it does help to speak your dreams. You never know, someone who might be able to help you realize them will hear you! If you are not willing to sacrifice for your dreams, then it may not happen. You have to want them to come true. Taking no for an answer should not deter you. You may need to take a break from pursuit of your dreams to put food on the table and a roof over your head, but never give up! Your dreams are sacred. Be patient. Success does not happen overnight. Don't be afraid to ask for help, but never expect someone to make your dream come true for you. It's up to you! Look for a mentor. I am always happy to help young photographers when asked. Find your passion, find your bliss.

— Rich Cruse (age fifty-three)

WORTHY STRIDES

For a purpose, I'm gonna run—
Been training for months.
This obstacle, I will overcome.
Working out with so much vigor,
Because even though the obstacle is big,
My dreams are even bigger.
Physically, I've been in pain.
Mentally, strength I've gained.
The gun sounds, and I'm off to the races.
My heart is beating out of my chest,
The adrenaline, I'm embracing.
My whole life people always told me why I "can't,"
But crossing that finish line, I can.
I'm strides away from my realizing my dream,
until it turned into a nightmare accompanied by screams…

Condolences to those killed and injured during the
Boston Marathon bombing

In order to keep your dreams safe, you have to take risks.

— Jean Clervil

Is my dream worth it? Honestly I am in a place where I don't know. When you pursue something for so long without success, you tend to question your level of sanity. May 14, 2015, literally marked a ten-year pursuit toward a career I haven't been successful in. On the ninth year, I questioned whether I was living the wrong dream. I wanted to know what God desires and dreams for me. See, with me, after such a long time of chasing dreams of what people had for me, I realized that the Lord has jokes. He is a clever God. He strategically placed people in my life to encourage and to push me. Gem after gem was being dropped in front of me, and I was ignoring precious stones for gravel. After ten years I have come to the conclusion that I have been insane with the desire to satisfy man and not God. The moment I came to that realization, things got even harder. I wanted to go back to the dream of becoming a nurse. I wanted to go back to living up to that standard that everyone put me on. I began to struggle with my faith because I questioned whether I'd wasted all of my time on the wrong dream because it hadn't manifested yet. The constant reminder that I wasn't a nurse slapped me in the face every day I stepped into work and saw coworkers younger than me becoming nurses while I'm still in clerical servitude. A constant reminder that my bills superseded my wages because I wasn't a nurse made me bitter and unenthusiastic. What I thought would put me in a position to provide for others and myself didn't happen as planned. How can ten years' worth of knowledge go to waste? How can all of the things that I know be put to use? Why am I teaching nurses how to perform policy and procedure when I can be doing so much more? I must admit, the sting of not "making my dream come true" after ten years burned like leather seats in the summer. Between my financial-aid debt and planning for a wedding, I was more stressed than ever. So I question myself knowing that I don't want to be here. Amid my mental warfare and questioning my sanity, something clicked. Why I am following my own path and not God's path?

Each time that I can recall a roadblock to my pursuits, it was always something that had minimal to do with me. And it didn't click until I wrote an essay to apply for graduate school. It was at this point that I realized that a dream to me was nothing more than listening to God in prayer. Focusing solely on Christ was what I needed to do. There wasn't anything discussed about me not becoming a nurse ever, but right now it's not for me. My steps have been reordered for me. God is dreaming something more and creating an avenue for my full potential. I spoke with nurses at work about their dream and each and every one of them stated they had degrees in other areas. That was just confirmation that I followed the flesh dream. How selfish of me. No wonder it felt like insanity. No wonder it felt like it was my fault, because it was. I applied to graduate school on a whim without any financial security, car, or experience in the field. I took a leap of faith. The application to graduate school was on my heart in 2011, but I refuted it to pursue the flesh dream. These two scriptures keep coming to my head:

In nothing be anxious; but in everything by prayer and supplication with thanksgiving let your requests be made known unto God. The things which ye both learned and received and heard and saw in me, these things do: and the God of peace shall be with you.
(Philippians 4:6, 9)

Look straight ahead with honest confidence; don't hang your head in shame. Plan carefully what you do, and whatever you do will turn out right. Avoid evil and walk straight ahead. Don't go one step off the right way. (Proverbs 4:27)

So you asked me what does my dream mean to me and is it worth it? (Chuckles) I don't know anymore. Or maybe I do, because the dream isn't mine to follow. I dream of living an abundant life in peace. And I'm grateful that I have friends, family, and a fiancée that's there to walk with me along the way.

— *Claudia Brunson (age twenty-eight)*

CAN I?

What if I can't find the money I need?
What if I can't find the right job?
What if I can't pay these bills?
What if I can't make these ends meet?
What if I can't turn this nightmare into a dream?
What if I can't turn this obstacle into an opportunity?

But what if you *can*?

*If I were to ask you for a description of your cell phone, you'd be able to tell me everything from its color to your favorite feature. How? Because we think in pictures. Now, if I were to ask you to describe what a day of you living your dream would look like... what would you see? Most people don't have a clear picture of their dream because they let **FEAR** hold the camera. The reason that imagination is more important than knowledge is because it has no limits. Visualize, because what you see is what you get.*

*— **Jean Clervil***

I NEVER KNEW

Never could've afforded a watch,
So I never knew when my time was coming.
Spent my last dollar on a dream.
Now I can't afford to sleep.
This patient ran out of patience,
And now I can't afford medication.
When things don't go right,
I go write...

Are your gifts currently being utilized in your area of work?
YES | NO

In all honesty, it all simply comes down to a feeling. If you've ever spoken to someone who truly believes that they've found their calling, their energy immediately engulfs you. If you pay attention, you can clearly see and feel that said person truly believes in what they're doing and is willing to sacrifice anything to get even a step closer to their (what I like to call) personal success. I, on the other hand, am quite successful (by society's standards for success, different from "personal success") for someone my age. But I have no passion for what I'm doing. I have no deep pride for my work. I'm not excited when I wake up each morning truly believing I've found my calling. What's worse is that I work with many people twice my age making even more than myself and you can see how the light has left their eyes. They've become drones simply going with the motions, helping someone else achieve their dream having let go of theirs seemingly a lifetime ago. In a lot of way it's incredibly dangerous for a person with big goals like myself to be spending so much time in that kind of environment, but there are some benefits which can't be ignored. Having said that, every day I pray, read, speak to people, research, anything I can do to try and awaken that burning passion I know lives deep within me because I'll be damned if I live the rest of my life shackled to someone else's dream.

— Joshua Joseph (age twenty-six)

"*Pay attention to your intuition so that you can receive a full ride to the life of your dreams.*"

— *Jean Clervil*

FEAR LESS

I'm not fearless; I just decided to fear less.
My dreams manifested when I gave my doubts a rest.
It's not that I'm not in pain; we all are—I just embrace it.
I looked in the mirror at my fear and faced it.
It's not that I don't get stuck,
I just learned to follow my gut.
It's not that I always know *how*, I just know my *why*.
When I felt like quitting is when I knew that success was nearby.

That moment that you felt like quitting, did your reason(s) why flash before your eyes and stop you?
YES | NO

I read an article about a pastor of a mega church in New York who is also the football coach of the local Jesuit high school. He said, "On Monday morning, most of my congregation will have forgotten what I preached about Sunday, but my players will never forget the lessons I teach because they are in pain when I teach them." This article resonated with me because as a high-school wrestler, I remember, very clearly, the pain of up and downs, suicides, and takedown drills during practice. Our coach would repeat the mantra "Pain is temporary; pride is forever," and boy, did he put that one to the test. Today, I am a successful professional speaker, author, humorist, and radio personality and draw heavily on the pain I experienced from the numerous rejections I endured throughout my life. As a young Nashville songwriter, I was thrilled when I found out that Casey Kasem was to be at the conference I was attending. I, like all kids of the '80s, knew Casey Kasem not only as the voice of the top-forty countdown, but as the voice of Shaggy on Scooby Doo. I cajoled the person in charge to allow me to be the one to escort Casey Kasem and his wife in the golf cart across the hotel grounds. I started a conversation with him that ended up with me handing him a demo of my latest music. That brief encounter led to a meeting a few weeks later with the head of A & R for Curb Records. As I sat there in her office, I recalled all of the times that I had pitched songs to various publishers and record labels only to be told I wasn't good enough, or worse, ignored all together. Now I was sitting in the office of the person who could make my dreams come true because one of the biggest names in music had recommended me... this was my shot. She sat there listening to my three-song demo with a face devoid of expression. I began to fantasize about the different Curb Records artists that would be singing my songs. She turned off the player, looked at me, and said, "These songs are good, but let me tell you about a hit song. A hit song has a quality that makes the listener want to get up, drive to the CD store (remember those?), and pay fifteen dollars just to hear it again. These songs are good, but they are not hits." I couldn't believe what I was hearing. The pain from this rejection was bigger than any before. I walked out of that office more dejected than I had ever been, but in hindsight, it was a turning point for me. It was then that I decided to start writing songs for me based on what I liked, not what I thought a publisher would like. I realized that even though mainstream country music wasn't recording funny songs, I started writing comedy because I was good at it. The rejection that I experienced as a songwriter forced me to find my authentic self. I now am played daily on the SiriusXM Radio Family Comedy Channel, Laugh USA, and Blue Collar Radio and make more money from music than I ever did writing for a publisher. Like fingers on a hot stove, the pain we experience in life can guide us to becoming the person we are meant to be.

— Patrick Henry (age forty-three)

"Count your blessings and you'll lose count of your misfortunes."

— *Jean Clervil*

PLEASE SEND MY CONDOLENCES

They say death comes in threes.
Personally, I didn't think I could handle all of the RIPs.
First, I'd like to send my condolences to my fear of failing.
I can't walk on water if I'm afraid of sailing.
Second, I'd like to send my condolences to someone I loved
dearly.
RIP to the person that I used to be.
See, this is more than an elegy.
But lastly, I'd like to send my condolences to…

Work > Wish

To wish for something isn't enough, you have to be willing to work for it.

The question of "Is it worth it?" to me is one that can never fully be answered. I'll never know if competing for five years was "worth it"; similarly, law school is a means to an end that may or may not be justified in ten, twenty, or fifty years. Everyone undertakes initiatives operating under the assumption that the goal is worth it, or else we would all be doing nothing. In short, it's a question that has to be yes in the present tense, and has no concrete answer looking retrospectively. Perhaps it is not the correct question at all. The answer of current worthiness is always yes, and actions must evolve in constant reevaluation of the steps taken to accomplish or achieve something. Or else I would have never started, never continued, never planned for any form of future life. You can't accurately determine the future value of any decision today. Quite honestly, you still may never know the value of it at the point of maturity. I'm sure one of the many questions people in their last days ask is if something that utilized their energy was worth it. And I would argue that even they find no solace in selecting an answer because to acknowledge something as unworthy is forsaking the time and effort expended to that point, any lessons learned by decisions made, any life deviations that occurred in pursuit, and self-awareness gained in the process. So I cannot, and may never be able to, objectively answer the question "Is it worth it?" because humanity only exists in the present, and our actions are dictated by an internal qualification system that makes millions of decisions a day to do the more worthy activity. This could be one of my idiosyncrasies, or a characteristic of the masses, but I believe that to live a purpose-driven life, it is categorically impossible to deem any current action unworthy.

— Jachelé Vélez (age twenty-five)

SO WHY WOULD YOU?

You ever try to feed someone who wasn't hungry?
You ever try to give someone water who wasn't thirsty?
You ever try to shed light to someone who didn't even know
that he or she was in the dark?
You ever try to chase someone who didn't want to be caught?
You ever try to find someone who wasn't lost?
...So why would you try to share your vision with someone who
only has sight?

Do you seek counsel from a mentor?
YES | NO

"*The math is easy, subtract people who don't add value to your life.*"

— *Jean Clervil*

*As a young black male living in the suburbs of Philadelphia, I always wanted to be a police officer. I always looked at it as a noble career and my perceptions of them was that they were the leaders of the community that kept everyone safe. This changed once I attended undergraduate school and my experience with police officers was the complete opposite. On multiple occasions I was harassed by police officers in West Chester, Pennsylvania. The harassment ranged from unwarranted pullovers to police officers pinning charges, assuming I was in a gang (there are no gangs in the suburbs in Philadelphia). This led to me changing my major from criminal justice to philosophy. I didn't want anything to do with studying about or having a career in law enforcement. Graduating with a degree in philosophy and losing hope in the criminal justice system, I had no idea what I wanted to do as a career. Six months after graduating, I started as a behavioral health worker at a middle school in North Philadelphia. Because I was born and raised in the suburbs, I was blind to the poor educational conditions and how what young people were going through in the inner city. Working with youth in North Philly is where I found my dream. I went from behavioral health work to becoming a special education teacher in a matter of months and I began to love my students as if they were my own children. Unfortunately, I was laid off because of budget cuts after a year, but that didn't kill my dream. While I was laid off, I spearheaded a mentoring program at Overbrook High School, which is my alma mater. I mentored young men between ninth and twelfth grade. My mentoring included social and academic after-school programming, which were "Man Up," Homework Club, Reading Club, and Fitness Friday. My undying love and passion for working with urban youth continued to grow. With my passion I founded a youth organization in 2012, **The Philadelphia Youth Project**. The organization's mission is to engage, encourage, and* *educate youth in Philadelphia through community events, life-skills workshops and educational events. I started this organization trying to help the youth grow from the issues they may be at risk of. I am currently employed as an educator at Youth Build Philadelphia Charter School. Youth Build Philadelphia Charter School offers out-of-school youth, ages eighteen to twenty, a second chance to earn a high-school diploma and prepare for college and career. Working at Youth Build is an extremely fulfilling opportunity. I look at it as more than a "job"; it's like a second home. I take advantage of the ability to be able to work with youth and to impact communities by doing community work with youth as often as possible. I develop and cherish the relationships that I have with the young men at Youth Build because of my relationship with my father, which isn't the greatest. Because I don't get paid as much as I wish, I'm always asked if my career path is worth it and the answer is always "without a doubt." I was once in court supporting one of my students who was potentially getting sentenced for drug charges and in a disgruntled tone, the judge asked me, "Why do you work with this kid?" And to return her energy, I arrogantly answered, "If I don't, then who will? And I'm sure you have no interest in doing so!" My passion for urban youth will never die.*

— Christopher McFadden (age twenty-nine)

NONRENEWABLE

If you're not passionate about it,
you're wasting your time.
If you're keeping tabs on the clock,
you're wasting your time.
If you're comfortable while doing it,
you're wasting your time.
If no one is discouraging you,
you're wasting your time.
If you had a fuck and gave it,
you're wasting your time.
If you read this and weren't inspired,
I've wasted my time.

Are you wasting your time?
YES | NO

Every ounce of pain that I've endured while chasing my dream has been worth it. It has always been my dream to use the gifts that God has blessed me with to help uplift the lives of others. What kind of person would I be to ignore the dreams that He instilled in me? Every ounce of pain that I've endured is nothing compared to the glory that follows. The pain of not reaching my full potential, the pain of not being everything I've been put here to be is the worst pain I know. Being put on earth and not fulfilling my purpose is the pain that I fear the most. I believe that a life without dreams is no life at all.

— *Ahmed Annan (age twenty-five)*

SHARE

Imagine a form of communication where
you don't have to worry about having no service,
where you aren't restricted to one hundred forty characters,
where you don't have to tap to retry,
where your message won't go in spam,
where your thoughts won't be exposed to the world.
Well, there is such a form of communication available,
and it's called prayer.

Do you pray?
YES | NO

It's 10/30/2014, 4:00 this morning I was awaken out of my sleep, and decided to pray, read, and meditate. As I am on my knees crying and praying, asking God for direction and guidance as I am feeling frustrated. Recently I became a supervisor at my job, I am on three different committees within my fraternal organization, a graduate student, and newly engaged. Needless to say, these are all things I asked God for; however, as the saying goes, "To whom much is given, much is required." I am out of my comfort zone, and it's forcing me to be stretched and extend myself more than ever. Even though I feel like throwing in the towel, I know I can't quit. I know what my ultimate goal of being a clinical psychologist as well as a business owner of my own social services company will become a reality. However, the experiences that I am going through now, the "it" which is the pain, the frustration, and being uncomfortable are part of the process. Success doesn't come overnight, and the feelings that I am experiencing are natural. How I perceive my situation is on me: I can look at it as defeat or as growth. Holding on to my vision, and knowing the plan God has for me is bigger than my experience and the best is yet to come. So yes, I know it is worth it, more than I can see at this present moment. "Faith is the substance of things hoped for, and the evidence of things not seen" (Hebrews 11:1).

— Theodore Peterson (age thirty)

"Things started working when I stopped worrying."

— *Jean Clervil*

A CONVERSATION WITH GOD

So I sit here confined by my thoughts,
And as I blink, I think of how life could be...
But what I see isn't seen;
What I feel isn't felt
By anyone else but me.
They say to whom much is given, much is tested.
Well, can you hand me a cheat sheet, 'cause this shit got me
    stressing.
Every day I awake, you say, is a blessing.
But to awake to reality that I feel is fake
Makes my heart ache and my mind quake.
You say death and life lie in the tongue,
But as I speak my words into existence,
I feel as though your eardrums are numb.
I've heard that you're never too late and always on time.
I know you hear my cries; I know you see my sighs.
But I can only ask why?
How can I discipline my disappointment
when with success I can barely schedule an appointment?
A child of God I am; a product of this world I refuse to be.
But I surrender and shall stand still and watch you work within
    me.
I've been resistant, and for success I am persistent.
I'm not losing faith; I'm just losing patience.
I am ill, so please supply medication for this patient.
It took a while for me to believe in myself, and believe me—I do.

I've been doing all I can and more, so I'm leaving the rest unto
    You.
You gave me the gift of words that I can use to change lives,
So now I am using the weapons you gave me to kill myself
In order to live a new life....
Wait—I see images of what you have in store for me,
But when I open my eyes, I see nothing in the inventory...
I mean, even Jesus was stoned before receiving the throne.
And I, as I close my eyes, see that I'm already home.
This is really personal—better yet, soulful.
You created me in your image, and I feel it developing in front of
    my eyes.
It's just that I have to be more patient and allow the real You in
    me to arise....

IM CALLING OUT

He works full time, but we give him part-time credit.
Some don't even believe that He clocks in at all.
Unsatisfied by the surface,
We try to confront him, believing that at times
He doesn't listen.
He does more than we see,
Accomplishes more than we comprehend.
You can't fire your coworker, let alone your boss.
But if you work with God, He'll work for you.

SUBPOENA

Today, my dreams received a subpoena,
And it read that my faith must stand trial.
Ironic, because I've already been tried and tested.
Challenges and setbacks have become the norm.
How can I discipline my disappointment
when with success I can barely schedule an appointment?
I entered the courtroom and faith represented me,
but the jury was filled with my doubts...

The moment you doubt, you cancel your blessing.

— *Gerald Highsmith*

Dreams are never materialized without hard work and dedication. Dreamers must be willing to pursue their vision at all cost. It's the obstacles encountered that make us stronger. I have learned from the lives of others as well as myself that the pains endured through my struggles have been the fuel that has kept me pushing. No great thing comes without great struggle. If it were possible to just sit back and wait for it to happen, we would all be living our dream. Dream chasers are those who understand that the life they have been given is designed to impact the world. They realize that the purpose for their lives is to push themselves and others into Destiny. Most of the pain I have experienced has been internal: doubt, fear, and loneliness, to name a few. I have had to constantly remind myself that greater is he who is within me. I now live my life to show others the gifts that lie within themselves. So yes, it is worth it.

— Ron Brangman (age forty-four)

IT DOESNT MAKE SENSE

"I put my heart and my soul into my work and have lost my mind
    in the process."
Van Gogh sure must've known.
I wanted to receive the gift of success,
So I paid the price.
But every day, reality questions whether my purchase was right.
I've invested in a vision that would even make Stevie Wonder.
My fear is frangible,
And I lost my mind once I found out that
I was holding on to something intangible...

You ever hear an adult tell you about their regrets and their what-ifs?
It's sad. You can read the confusion on their face and the loss in their
eyes. No matter what they've accomplished they're still caught up in the
what-if. I never wanted to have that. Everyone has fears, but I never
wanted my fears to define my reality. I experienced loss in many ways
as a teenager into young adulthood that made me realize you have to
take advantage of the time you have. You have to be fearless about your
endeavors,
especially if you feel your destiny looming around you.
It is so easy to be negative. Most of us have warped ideas of reality
and dreams. I decided that my dreams were going to be a reality. My
move to Los Angeles was scary in thought but exciting in actuality. I
knew I would have to struggle and I was prepared to have no friends/
support, but I was positive about this. I addressed both scenarios with
patience and understanding that if that became a reality, it wouldn't
last for long. The beauty of taking the leap of faith is the stretching you
endure mentally and even physically. If I had stayed in fear, I would
be stuck in the muck of complacency and monotony intentionally. Call
me a dare devil or a free spirit, but if I fall, I know God has my back.
Determination. Faith. And Desire. My advice to you, soul-searching,
on the brink of taking that leap, is to see beyond your eyes and prepare
yourself for the work. Overcoming a fear isn't easy. Overcoming fear is
growth. It is exciting if you address it with love, dedication, and positive
thought.

— Tremana White (age twenty-six)

RISKY

I realize what I cherish the most.
I'll risk my money for its increase.
I'll risk my time for its future worth.
I'll risk my sanity for what doesn't make sense.
I'll risk my life to make history,
but I haven't risked what I seem to cherish the most—my heart.
See...

Hell, yeah, my dream is worth it! What's the point of living if you're not dreaming or pushing yourself to be a better you? Life is more than paying bills and Sallie Mae. Being alive is blessing in itself, but why not get more out of it? Dreaming keeps me alive; I will forever be a dreamer. I will turn my dream(s) into my reality. Being a creative is who I am, so dreaming comes natural. Yeah, the pain, sweat, and tears are worth it all for me. To me, that's part of the process. Nothing great comes easy. It's like working out or getting in shape, you know it's real when you're feeling the burn—that's growth. If everything comes easy, then you should be scared. Trust me, the pain can be discouraging at times, but you never know your potential if you stop at a roadblock. You have to use adversity as your fuel and go that much harder. This is something I'm learning every day. You only live once, so don't regret not doing what you love.

— **Moruf Adewunmi (age twenty-seven)**

ROAD LESS TRAVELED

A nomad, in no man's land—
Well, no sane (wo)man, at least—
Traveling down a road where my faith is supposed to decrease,
Where my dreams are supposed to be deceased,
Where doubt stays in my head without paying rent or a lease.
Willingly I took this road less traveled,
Carrying luggage that I'm supposed to handle.
And even though my sanity is being tested,
My faith is being proven.

Have you ever felt like quitting?
YES | NO

I find this to be such a heavy question, but it has such a simple answer. Yes! My dreams are worth it. When you asked me this, all of the struggles and hardships that I've faced on my journey and continue to face to this day flashed before my eyes. Fortunately enough, I'm at a place now where I can reflect on them positively because I know, without a shadow of a doubt, that I was built for the path I'm on and that everything I face along the way is only intended to prepare me for the next phase. It took me twenty-three years to find my path. I was someone who, from the outside looking in, probably appeared to have it all together. I come from a great family who loves and supports me. I got a good education. I played sports my whole life and throughout college. I was somewhat popular with the ladies (at least in my mind), and I stayed out of trouble. I was never really told that I couldn't do something. In fact, everyone around me has always given me the whole "you can be or do anything you choose to" speech. My problem was that I never really knew who I wanted to be or what I wanted to do. I did many things to pass time, but there was never anything that I felt like I could make a life of. There were many points where I became depressed and overwhelmed by the pressure of living up to everyone's expectations for me. I was trying so desperately to please the world around me and I was putting my happiness on the back burner to do so. As my senior basketball season and college was coming to a close, I had to begin asking myself what the next step was. I didn't have a plan. Up until that point, I was living as if scholarships, meal plans, and dorm rooms would always have my back. The real world didn't seem real to me. The last day of your last semester has a way of putting everything in perspective, though. I decided I was going to work all summer and move to California the fall after college. I had no idea what I was going to do, but I knew that I had some good friends in Los Angeles, and I was dying to make a move. I had always had a longing to live there, and I just felt like it was the place for me. I knew that I was done with basketball, and

*I needed to search for myself. I needed to find my path. The thought of packing up my car and driving across the country with no set plans gave me all the energy I needed that summer to work and save up money for my new life on the West Coast. I sold cars that summer at Volkswagen in Manchester, New Hampshire. I knew nothing about cars, and still don't, but my managers and sales team helped me tremendously. I just used my love and compassion for people and good conversation to convince customers that I wasn't out to empty their pockets, and it worked. I was making great money, and with each sale, California got closer and closer. Then it hit me. Trayvon Martin had just been killed, and the country began to divide in wake of the media's coverage. I was having intense conversations with my mother and two best friends, and we were just trying to figure out why this had happened. We wanted to understand what the underlying issue was. There was a problem that needed to be tackled. After countless hours of dialogue over the next couple of days, I found myself obsessed with the topic. I was angered by how easily everyone passed judgment on people that they had never met. I came to the conclusion that the biggest issue in the world is a lack of understanding and willingness to accept any reality that which is not our own. Then I asked myself, "What could you do about it?" That's when **I'm Just Different** came about. I began incorporating all of my interests and experiences into an idea for a movement to inspire individuality, understanding, and acceptance of differences. I had found my path. I can look back and pinpoint the exact day that I knew my life would never be the same. I didn't know how I would make this idea come to life, but I knew I would. The fall came, and I quit my job and moved to California with just a few dollars in my pocket and the promise of a floor to sleep on at a friend's place. I purchased a cheap air mattress, which soon developed a slow leak that would have me waking up on the floor with terrible pain in my back every morning. I struggled to find a job or some source of income for a good while. I* *found myself flat broke pretty early on and had to constantly call on the assistance of family and friends, many of which were not in a position to help, but they found a way simply out of love and their belief in what I was trying to accomplish. A few months in, I landed a job working the front desk at Equinox in West Hollywood. This gym was extremely star studded and allowed me to make lots of connections, although I was getting paid minimum wage. I did this for a couple of months until I landed a "big boy" job at a Lionsgate-owned television company as a marketing assistant. I got this job based on a referral from the first person that I met when I got to LA at a Subway near my friend's apartment. We spoke about our love for subs and he turned out to be the VP of programming at this particular company. We stayed in touch for months and when a job opened up, he gave me a call for an interview. I was super excited to finally have a solid income and to be in a position to escape the floor and an air mattress with a slow leak. Things appeared to be looking up for me. That is, until I realized that I was becoming a slave to a paycheck. I wasn't happy, and I knew it was because I wasn't doing what I set out to do in LA. I wasn't impacting the world from my cubicle. I felt as though I was shortchanging everyone that I believed who needed to hear my message and myself. The guilt became unbearable, and I quit with the support of my employer and everyone around me whom I reached out to for advice. I realized that I would never be happy working to achieve the dream of someone else if that meant that I had to put mine aside. I wasn't going to delay my dreams anymore. I made a vow to chase my dreams because I didn't see anyone else running after them. My dream and everything that has come along with it—the struggles, the pain, and the hardships—will just make my success story that much greater. I've lived to please other people, and I have failed many times. Now I'm living for my own approval, and I find that I haven't let myself down half as much, and when I do, I only have myself to blame. I can live with that. The past couple of years, there were so many ups and downs. There were so many points where I felt like giving up, but I always found the energy to keep pushing forward. In this time, I've met all types of people who have helped me turn my vision into what it is today. This path has brought me to some interesting places, and it's far from over, but I can look back on all that I've encountered while chasing this dream and say that I wouldn't change a single thing. I embrace the journey. I embrace the struggle. I embrace the pain.*

— *Lamont Stapleton (age twenty-six)*

When you worry, you put faith in the things that you don't want.

— *Jean Clervil*

YESTERDAY < TODAY

Yesterday I was broken, but today I am blessed.
Worry is a debt that I can no longer afford.
Negativity keeps knocking, but I won't open the door.
I prayed for patience when I should've prayed for endurance.
I asked for a quote to keep my dreams safe, and faith was the
    insurance.
This diamond needed pressure.
This seed needed water.
I graduated from struggle, and perseverance is my alma mater.
Yesterday I was broken, but today I am blessed.
I was broken and paralyzed; fear was the diagnosis.
In order for my story to be written, there had to be conflict.
In order for this movie to be produced, fear had to be the
    antagonist.
In order to keep my dreams safe, I had to take the risk.
Rain was made to fall on the just and unjust.
Life changed when I turned my "shoulds" into "musts."

I am a dreamer. It is what I have always done best. I spent childhood years with my imaginary "friends" and teenage years gazing out of windows during class envisioning all the pieces of my future that seemed so far ahead of me. But as we mature into adulthood, we tend to stop dreaming. We hit the pause button or we give up. I know that may sound negative but it is true. I know...because that was me. I always wanted to be a ballerina, but I grew up being told, "Dance is not a career, it is a hobby." So I stopped dreaming about being a dancer and treated what I loved most as a leisure pursuit. I gave up on my dream at the age of sixteen. And let's be real, we have all given up on a dream of ours at some point in this lifetime. But the beauty about any dream is that we only have the vision for it when it is aligned with our passion. So even when we "give up" on our dreams, passion never lets it die. I spent four years in college fighting against my passion, studying something other than dance because I was told that only failure would be there to greet me if I followed my dreams. I searched for auditions and castings daily, only to never actually go. But that moment comes in life when you grow so uncomfortable pretending, trying to fit your circle into life's square, that the only thing you feel in life is confusion. This became my life; where my passion ate away at me because my dreams were calling and I was not answering. For six years I suppressed my dream of being a performer before I unlocked the dream that I put away at sixteen and attended an audition that changed my life forever. My passion led me back to my dream that became a goal, to which I accomplished. In doing so, I learned that the hardest part about chasing my dream was not seeing it as an idea but as my objective and to believe that I held the power to achieve it. Achieving my dream to dance on a professional level pushed me to create new dreams...a dream to dedicate a school specifically to the arts. A school that helps young visionaries turn their dreams into real life accomplishments. Every painful second I continue to spend working towards my dreams will be priceless, because

I'll be one step closer to helping another young dreamer turn their dream into a reality. The painful moments of my journey will be worth it when I save the next young teen from making the mistake of giving up on their dreams too soon. Sometimes all we need is for someone to believe in us. And as a young dreamer who once searched for the very same thing, I know it is my job to be that for the next young person, that dreams that big yet attainable dream of becoming a ballerina.

— Chastity M. (age twenty-six)

GUT FEELING

A dream ignored turns into doubt.
An opportunity missed turns into an obstacle.
Ideas get wasted when action doesn't take place.
You're nuts if you don't follow your gut.
You're pregnant with possibilities.
You're potent with potential.
You want to schedule your appointment with success?
Learn to discipline your disappointments.
What you're waiting for
is waiting for you.
When you procrastinate, you tell your dreams to wait.

Are you excited to go to work today?
YES | NO

Hustle > Hope

Hope is not a strategy, action is.

Capture the moment.
Action cures fear and procrastination.
Reaping occurs only after you sow.
Plant your seeds today.
Each day should be invested, not spent.

Do not worry about tomorrow, for tomorrow will worry about itself.
Invest the 86,400 seconds given to you daily wisely.
Every day is a present, so don't hesitate to unwrap it.
Make your lives extraordinary.

"If your list of complaints is bigger than your list of blessings, obstacles will find you. If your list of blessings is bigger than your list of complaints, opportunities will find you. "

— Jean Clervil

THIS IS NOT WHAT I ASKED FOR

I asked for success
and received struggle.
I asked for love
and received heartbreaks.
I asked for opportunity
and ran into obstacles.
I asked for wisdom
but leaned on my own understanding.
I don't ask for much,
but what I receive afterward frustrates me so much.
Then I realized that
God is more interested in changing *me* than He is in changing
my circumstances.

THE WEALTHIEST PLACE ON EARTH

Let me tell you of a place
Where abundance occupies the space.
It is not in Africa, where you can find diamonds.
It is not in the Far East, where there is oil.
Yet, it is placed deep within nature's soil.
You need not look far to find its location.
Millions go there to take a permanent vacation—
A place where there are enough resources to leave legacies.
But none of them were discovered,
So now they are history.
The wealthiest place on earth is the cemetery,
Where the world's greatest talents, ideas, and abilities lay buried.
Potential is only energy standing still.
But for those who let fear overcome their will,
Like their bodies—their dreams remained still.
Many go to their grave with their ideas and talents
That the world never got a chance to be exposed to.
Now that they lay dormant.
Many believe that they can tiptoe through life
To gain a sense of security,
But in fact they risked nothing.
And to do so is the greatest jeopardy.
Do not let your impulse to dream die.
Do not let your right to wealth be denied.

A person doesn't die when he or she reaches the grave;
They die when their dreams do.
So instead let your dreams live and your fears die,
And continue in your pursuit.

Did you wake up this morning?
YES | NO

Sometimes I don't know what to think, so instead I just be.

Aware the world can become an intense place, but I won't let the world own me.

Broken society hiding what's inside of me,
they tell us we're in a free environment but we have to fight to be free.

So if I have to fight to be free—I will surely be wounded, but I will rise solely as me:
untouched, unconformed, and unruly.

Giving myself to the world before I sleep is pure goal, and that is why my purpose on ground's earth and heaven's skies manifests to be pure gold.

Enduring the world's weight on my shoulder in nothing.
Things that would make you colder make me warmer, closer to triumph.
It is the challenge that makes the accomplishments much more beautiful.

— Giselle Lopez (age twenty)

I found my passion and got lost in the right direction.

— Jean Clervil

Failure is seen by many as a complete loss. What's lost in this opinion is the value gained in pursuing your dreams. There is tremendous value in learning while you are reaching for your dreams even if you fall short. The key is to carefully measure the value of your dream path. Is making it part way more valuable than not trying at all? If so, you're likely on the right path and should go after this goal or dream. For example, I set out to publish at least one article every single day of 2015. Now well into the year, I have gained a following, been offered new opportunities, and improved my skills as a writer. Even if I fail to publish tomorrow and fall short of my dream, the journey will be worth it because of the value I've received. Not every dream is going to provide you value up front or each day you're working on it, but you have to appreciate the process and truly believe that even if you fail, the value gained will be worth the time you spent pursuing it. This doesn't mean you should take failing lightly or give up easily, but it does mean taking a step back and appreciating what you have learned and accomplished while doing what most people fail to do—going for it!

— Michael Luchies (age thirty)

"Your dreams won't take you seriously until you write them down."

— **Jean Clervil**

Inspired?
*Share a picture of your favorite poem, quote, and/
or testimony on social media using the hashtag*
#IsItWorthIt

IS IT WORTH IT?

*Y*ou and I have now reached the point where we have to decide whether what you're ~~going~~ growing through is worth it or not. The majority of the poems written in this book have a corresponding question following them. I came up with these questions as a measurable way to determine where you're at this very moment. Your answer to these questions will help you decide if what you're currently ~~spending~~ investing the majority of your time is worth it or not. Below I have written the significance of what you may have answered throughout the book. By the end of all of these questions, you'll be able to answer if your dream and the pain that comes along with it is worth it to you or not.

Are you currently willing to sacrifice the things you own to reach your goal?
YES | NO

YES: If you're willing to sacrifice what you have now to gain everything you yearn for later, then you're on the right track. I wrote "An Ode to Dreamers" when I felt like everything I tried to hold on to was literally holding me back: my old way of thinking, my old circle of friends, my old habits, and so forth. I realized that in order to receive the benefits of success, I had to pay the costs. Once I realized that, I started to change so that my circumstances could do so as well. Let me tell you—I was tired of not being able to put gas in my car. I was tired of coming up with lies to tell my wireless carrier so that they wouldn't cut off my phone. I was tired of not being able to participate in certain activities with my friends because I didn't have enough money to cover my own expenses. So the pain of that forced me to realize that I'm going to sacrifice what I need to until further notice—until I can create the opportunity for the lifestyle that I've been dreaming about.

NO: If you're not willing to sacrifice, you're sacrificing your dreams. Something has got to give. In order for you to gain something, you have to be willing to offer something for it. If you're not where you want to be *right now*, you have to give up something. And it is not simply material things. You have to sacrifice your old way of thinking and embrace what you have to change in order for new things to happen for you. If your answer is no, you're being lazy and don't deserve what you claim to want.

"Your goal shouldn't be proving people wrong, it should be proving yourself right."

— *Jean Clervil*

Is your reason why *big enough to stop you from quitting?*
YES | NO

YES: If your reason for *why* you must manifest this dream of yours is big enough to stop you from quitting, then that must mean that it's near and dear to your heart. No price can be put on your *why*. Money alone will not motivate you to overcome your biggest obstacle. Money should be a perk, not the purpose. I have many reasons why I won't quit. Besides the cliché of "being sick and tired of being sick and tired," my mom is my biggest motivation. She came from another island with a dream of making a better life for her and her son. She did everything that she needed to do to provide and never made an excuse for it. To this day, I'm convinced that it is embedded in my DNA to make things happen. This has inspired me to make sure that the rest of her life is the best of her life. There's nothing more satisfying than seeing the look on your parents' faces when they are proud of you. I could write multiple books on my reasons *why*. I shared a portion of my *why* because every time I face an obstacle, I see my mother's face and think of how she made the impossible possible, and that keeps me going. Do yourself a favor and write down your reason(s) *why* and keep it close to you. Write it down and make copies. Place in your wallet or purse. Place it on your vision board. Place it by the bathroom sink. Stick it to the refrigerator door if you need to—as long as it's placed somewhere that will remind you daily.

NO: If your *why* is not big enough, you are going to quit. It's that plain and simple. The moment you feel like quitting, you're going to ask yourself, "WHY am I doing this?" Pictures of your *why* will flash in front of your very eyes, and if your *why* is not **BIG** enough, you will give up.

Are you uncomfortable with where you're at?
YES | NO

YES: The most dangerous place on this earth is your comfort zone. By asking this question, I'm trying to help you figure out if you have stepped out of your comfort zone, because that's the only place where you can grow. You can't keep doing things the same way and expect new results. You have to step out and try to do something new every day. Find a new hobby, meet somebody new, or try a new approach to manifest that dream. As painful as it will be at first, you will be forever grateful at the new things and blessings that you discover.

NO: If you answered no, you've admitted that you are in your comfort zone and are OK with how things are at this very moment. If you answered no, let me personally tell you that you are in a very dangerous place. Playing it safe is dangerous. Every success-ful person you may look up to is constantly fighting to do some-thing new and trying his or her best to achieve something new. The moment you stop having goals is the moment you stop giving yourself something to live for.

I feel the pain is worth it chasing this dream of mine to become one of the most creative persons of all time through visuals. It is worth losing sleep, losing friends and family members. I come from a city where you are praised for being an athlete, respected as a hustler, or feared as a gang member. Either way it's a process to becoming something more, good or bad. We often are afraid to become more because we have been given and shown less. So when given the chance to see different, do different, and be so-called different, our culture gives us the hand to the face because we aren't following the socially cultural normal path that was shown to us. This is my whole reasoning that I do not mind the pain because we were born into the pain already. So pain isn't the issue because it is already going to happen. While in pain, I've endured and accepted it. I have accepted the struggle; I have accepted the lonely nights creating while friends party or studying for years just so I can graduate college. Spending hours on my creativity is hard while my sick grandmother needs me in the next town. I constantly brainstorm to create my own path. It's hard missing out on seeing my son every day because I have to finish school and work and create a path of my own that I have never seen before. Pain is normal for me at least because it is expected. Without pain there is no gain. That doesn't just go for working out the body; that goes for working through this process experience we call life. My reason for not stopping is that when the pain is gone, I will be given more than I have worked for. My son will see and know what real dedication and hard work is without a sport, gun, or a corner. My family will see their first male graduate become a billionaire. Children of color will see me as someone who was dedicated that came from the same city they now live in. I am that little boy who wondered how Mommy got us gifts knowing she was broke. My why is to shape a generation of dreamers, believers, creators, and doers to look at themselves and ask, "Why not?"

— Joe V. Moore (age twenty-four)

Has anyone ever discouraged you from manifesting your dream?
YES | NO

YES: I ask this question during every one of my speeches. You have an idea, a vision, and an eagerness to manifest that picture you've painted in your head into your reality. We've all made the mistake of being overly excited at the birth of our newly found idea and wanting to share it with the first person we see and everyone else. Your dream will be tested. People will laugh at you. People will deter you. People will call you crazy. I've been called crazy so many times that I actually believe it and embrace it. Use every ounce of discouragement to encourage you, because no one can see your vision the way you see it. That's why it was given to *you*. Something has been placed in you that needs to be shared with the world, and everyone is not going to get it at first. Everyone is going to question you in the beginning, but once you manifest that dream of yours, *everyone* is going to want to ask you *how* did you do it.

NO: If no one is discouraging you right now, that means that you're not doing anything. If no one is hating on you, that means you're not doing anything worth hating on. People love to hate on what they don't understand. Crazy people are the only ones who truly succeed. Sane people are the ones who are satisfied with average. Sane people are always the first to quit.

Turn your dreams into a reality and that reality into a salary.

— Scott Mckenzie

Would you still do what you love to do for free?
YES | NO

YES: The gift you possess is an ability to do something so uniquely that no one else can do it the way you do it. Right now, think of what you really love to do. In fact, you are already doing it because when you are using your gift, you do it effortlessly. I write poems every time the thought of something new comes to me. I make people laugh because I enjoy it. I inspire people because it is a passion. I will continue to do these things until I take my last breath. In fact, I've been doing these things for free because they come naturally. The hardest thing for this generation to figure out is how to get compensated for the things you love to do. But you must be passionate about it first. Money follows passion. Money is attracted to passion. If you chase the money without the passion, you'll be running that race for a very long time.

NO: There will come a time when you realize your worth and put a price on your service. But in the beginning, you have to muster up enough belief in yourself that validates that price. We have heard countless times successful people saying that they would still do what they do if they were not getting paid for it. But for those who hear that and say, "It's easy for them to say because they already have the money," you have to realize the power of your gift. If you're not willing to do what you love for free, then you don't really love it. Your gift will make room for you, but you have to embrace it. Take the time to figure out what you really love to do. Someone will cut you a check for the things that you love to do for fun—just look at any profession. And if your dream job isn't available, create it. It's not empty pockets that stop people from living their dreams—it's empty minds that do. The economy won't affect your income, but your philosophy will.

*Once you prove how **valuable** you are, you'll never depreciate.*

— Jean Clervil

Are your gifts currently being utilized in your area of work?
YES | NO

YES: Whenever I did actually have a job, I was sure to let my light shine. When I worked for Foot Locker and Nike, I let my personality shine into an affable sales associate. When I was an orientation leader at William Paterson University, I led freshmen with my passion for learning more. When I was scooping italian ice for Rita's, I knew that accompanying my services with a smile made a huge difference. Although none of these jobs were my ideal job, I did what I had to do, but most importantly I learned what I had to learn. Every obstacle I went through served a purpose. Find out what you are meant to learn from your current situation and move on. Every single thing that I've learned from my previous jobs, I've been able to apply to my dream job of writing and inspiring the world.

NO: If you're a people person, you should be in front of people. If you're an artist, you should be creating art. If you're a problem solver, you should be creating solutions. You may not be working where you want to work right now, but you have to take something from it while you're still there. Meet whomever you have to meet. Learn whatever you have to learn. Do whatever you have to do now, and then go where your gifts are appreciated and valued.

I'm not sure if I'm still in pursuit of my calling. I think I tell myself that because the memories of my dreams burn in my brain. But if I were still in the pursuit of my dreams, I believe that I would have made some sort of progress than I have. Although it's hard admitting it, my current job puts a damper on chasing my dreams. It's the biggest interference of my life. I literally feel lost because of this. I want and have a need to pursue my passion, but my parents don't get it. I'm truly unhappy. I didn't even know feelings like this could exist with a job. I honestly want to take some type of part-time job just to have some income but to really have my freedom back. It just hit me: I am a servant to my job and do whatever they need from me. I would love to quit because my dream is burning me up, but the advice I get from people is that they think it's best to stay until you have a plan B. But if I start looking for a plan B, do I ever finish plan A?

*— **Kyla Womack (age twenty-six)***

That moment you felt like quitting, did your reason(s) why flash before your eyes and stop you?
YES | NO

YES: I cannot stress the importance of figuring out the reason *why* you want make the dream of yours come true. In my opinion, it is the most important factor in helping fight through the pain. At this point in the book, I hope that you have taken the time to write down your *why*. When I made the decision to self-publish my first book of poetry during my junior year in college, I sought advice from a teacher I favored. He bluntly told me that I was wasting my time. That shit hurt. It was bad enough that I was already a broke college student trying to realize my dream, but even worse, the person I thought would support me didn't. The moment that teacher discouraged me, all I could see was my mother's face along with the obstacles I was hell-bent on overcoming. I was so stubborn in my belief that doors opened where there were once walls. Weeks later, members of my church and friends held a fund raiser without my knowing, giving me the money I needed for publishing. Shortly after that, the same book that I was discouraged to write was in the university bookstore for sale and in the library for borrowing.

NO: If your *why* doesn't flash before your eyes and stop you, that means that your *why* isn't big enough. This also means that you may quit. Quitting is the easy way out. The only thing you should quit is wasting time. Take time out to discover what you love to do and spend time doing it. After that, write down *why* you can't spend another day not working toward the manifestation of this dream. The more you write down your *why*, the more you get emotionally attached to your dream. The more you get emotionally attached, the more unstoppable you become. Anything worth living for is worth fighting for. If your dream is worth it, you'll fight through the pain. If it is not worth it, you'll be defeated by it.

It's not over when you lose; it's over when you quit.

— Jean Clervil

Do you seek counsel from a mentor?
YES | NO

YES: If you are privileged enough to have a mentor to help guide you, please continue to keep that relationship healthy. The relationship between you and your mentor should be give-give. As a mentor is taking the time out to help you potentially grow your business, you should be seeking ways to be beneficial to him or her as well—in any way. The least that you can do is take the time to show appreciation. It really is the thought that counts. Remember birthdays, give a thank-you card, or write a heartfelt letter if you'd like. The more a mentor feels appreciated, the more he or she will be willing to help you. Another key to keeping the relationship with your mentor strong is to actually apply the information he or she is giving to you. Nothing will annoy a mentor more than taking the time to give someone he or she cares about information and then having the mentee deliberately ignore it and ask for advice again. Your mentor will feel like he or she is wasting time with you. If you ever disagree with a plan of action or anything else, express it and deal with it then. But all in all, keep the relationship healthy.

NO: You can't see the picture while you're in the frame. A mentor is someone already successful in his or her field of work who is willing to help and guide you. If you've answered no, then you clearly don't have a mentor, but you should take the time to find one. A mentor will help cut the learning curve. A mentor has already made the majority of the mistakes so that you won't have to. Your mentor could be closer to you than you know, but you have to take the time to find one. Network, and go to different places and events you've never been to before. Once you believe you've found your mentor, be honest and let him or her know that you would like him or her to help you. What do you have to lose?

Are you wasting your time?
YES | NO

Everything in the poem "Nonrenewable" is self-explanatory.

Firstly, if your dream and the pain that comes along with it isn't worth it to you, then what you have is not a dream but merely a goal. A dream encompasses passion and purpose. Anything short of compromising the integrity of who you are should be worth your "dream." In addition, if one looks at challenges and obstacles on the way to a dream as negative experiences, their mentality is flawed. All steps toward your dream are lessons. Many times our failed attempts are where we learn the most. You learn of the intestinal fortitude you possess, and you become wiser from your mistakes. The failed attempts are as much a part of the dream as the successful ones. I personally believe these lessons are the only thing of real value.

— **Dante Callahan (age twenty-five)**

Do you pray?
YES | NO

YES: I have been raised to be a God-fearing man. I've been enrolled in Catholic schools most of my life. Forcing religion down my throat didn't make me any closer to God. It wasn't until I took the initiative to seek him out myself that my life changed. If you have answered yes, then clearly you have and are working on your own unique relationship with him. Throughout the later poems in this book, you can see how I leaned on God when all else had failed. I've expressed my doubt, my frustration, and my worries. I've even questioned him: "WHY am I ~~going~~ growing through all this shit?" As I've mentioned in more than one poem, I realized that God is more interested in changing *me* than he is my circumstance. I've learned through prayer that every single thing that I've asked for, I was being prepared for. There's a difference between praying for something and being prepared to receive it. And if I haven't received it, then either I'm not ready for it or else it's not meant for me in the form in which I've asked for it. To me, prayer is simply a conversation with God. Prayer isn't always a reminder of how badly I need help; at times, it's just a moment to tell God how I'm doing and how grateful I am. I once heard that "prayer is talking to God, and inspiration is God talking back to you." Once you get off your knees, be prepared to move your feet and get moving. If you pray with any ounce of doubt, you've done it in vain. If you pray and are not willing to work for what you've asked for, you're simply begging. So continue to grow your relationship with God, because I believe that we are all destined for something greater than us. You are an idea away from living the life of your dreams, but when it comes to you, act on it.

NO: For those who have answered no, I am not here to convert you. I'm just sharing what has worked for me and what has kept my sanity going this long. I do believe that there is a higher power watching over me that has my back. Some call this higher power God, the Universe, Infinite Intelligence, and so forth. Whatever the case may be, do not think that you are in this alone. If you don't pray, try meditating. I would recommend taking some time to just be still and feel the energy that's around you. If you're feeling down, you have negative energy around you.

If you're feeling good, you have positive energy around you. Play your favorite song. Repeat affirmations with emotion. Exercise. Just take the time to find out what works for you. Do what makes you feel good so that it will attract more positive energy into your life. The more positivity you attract into your being, the more opportunities will find you attractive.

Have you ever felt like quitting?
YES | NO

YES: Everyone has felt like quitting at some point. Most do at the first sight of an obstacle. This question is aimed at those who feel like quitting at this very moment. The moment I shared my poetry with someone who didn't like it, I felt like quitting. When I published my first book and went months without a sale, I felt like quitting. When I went through months of not being booked as a speaker, I felt like quitting. However, it is in that very moment that I realized my *why* for doing so is much bigger than any obstacle that is placed in front of me. Your adversity serves a purpose. When you are meeting with resistance, it means that you are moving forward. Opportunities you enjoy today came from obstacles you overcame yesterday.

NO: If you haven't felt like quitting yet, that means you haven't striven hard enough. That means the goal that you've set out for yourself isn't big enough. If you haven't felt like quitting yet, prepare yourself, because the moment you make the decision to go after what you were born to do, obstacles will come in abundance to test how bad you really want it.

Don't break down; break through.

— Jean Clervil

The pain endured while traveling the road toward a dream is more than worth it. In life, especially in youth, there are desires. There are plans, and there are blueprints that we painstakingly design with bullets and milestones that we then relate to time. We often get so caught up in the attainment of said milestones in correlation to those dates, and when they don't match exactly, when the bullet misses the mark by a month or year, we lose focus. We second-guess ourselves. We start to negatively reevaluate. It's at that moment that we strip our goal of all its beauty. It's in the preoccupation with time that we blind ourselves and neglect to take stock in the lessons we are being given to prepare us for receipt of our goal/blessing, and it's in doing that that we make ourselves inept to handle it at all. I guess it's like being a child in the first grade who looks longingly at those in the sixth. If they focus so much on merely wanting to be in that position and envying those in it, they will miss out on all that's necessary to obtain. They'll be so ill prepared that once there, it will be nothing as they thought it would be, and even worse, depression will set in, daring them to ever have the audacity to dream again. The lessons from the pain are merit. They are the tools we use not only to get to that one point, but also to surpass it and graduate on to the next. It's in appreciating the lessons and taking time to reflect upon the beauty of the gem that we sometimes learn that the dream or goal we once set out to achieve is in fact the wrong one. Someone with tunnel vision fixed only upon achievement of that one goal might say that "no, none of it was worth it because I did not get what I thought I was putting my time into," whereas someone who has chosen to place the value in experience will say, "Yes, it was indeed worth the heartache to have learned this, because now, I can do so much more!" Personally speaking, my goal has only ever been happiness and love. Not exclusive to romance, but a happiness in and love for all things that I am tied to. Because of the inherent nature of that, I have to believe that there is purpose in all that I endure. I have to have faith that even when I set out to have something that I have convinced myself I want/need, if it should happen that I don't get it, then it was never for me, and thus, its necessity [is] disproved. That's not to say that not getting that thing doesn't hurt or that I'm in any way immune to disappointment. It's to say that those experiences teach me patience and resilience.

They teach me to hone in to my power of discernment. They teach me to be more critical and question why it is that I want something/someone. Why it is that I lend my energy to that thing or person. To me, understanding the "why" draws the "when" much closer and the "why not" makes it much sweeter. After all, I've heard several times in my life that it takes the experience of the storm to appreciate the rainbow.

— Laquia Norment (age twenty-nine)

Are you excited to go to work today?
YES | NO

YES: The evening before a speech, I can't sleep because I'm so excited. The afternoon leading into an open mic feature, I can't keep still. It's a high that would take some time to explain. When you are walking in your purpose—I mean, fully engulfed in it—you create your own energy. People always ask me, "Where do you get the energy from?" And I realize it's my passion that fuels me. It's a beautiful thing when you get paid for what you actually love doing. That's the only way that you will get excited to go to work, because at that point, it doesn't even feel like work anymore.

NO: Every day on social media, I see people I know complaining about work while at work. I see countless miserable selfies with captions like, "One more hour to go," "Can't wait till lunch," "Once I get out of here," and so forth. People will not hesitate to share their misery. We've all heard of the popular adage "misery loves company," but so does happiness. It's a beautiful thing to see people share about how they are actually excited about the day and the service they're rendering to the world. If your answer to this question is no, take the time to find out where your gift will be appreciated. Only that will begin to make you happy. Energy is contagious. People can sense when you do or don't want to be somewhere.

Did you wake up this morning?
YES | NO

YES: This is not a trick question. It is imperative that I get this point across to you. Follow these instructions with me: Take a deep breath and inhale. Now take a deeper breath and exhale. Do it again. Inhale and exhale. Now I need you to thank God that that wasn't your last breath. *You* are alive, while someone else is not. *You* can read this sentence, while someone else cannot. *You* are breathing at this very moment, while someone else just took his or her last breath. Time is of the essence, so how dare you waste it! The popular slogan "time is money" annoys the shit out of me. How dare someone compare the two when only one is irreplaceable! If I were to take anything that you own—including money—you could replace it. But if I were to take time from you, you couldn't get that back. Time is more valuable than money—period. Time is the only equal-opportunity employer. We all have the same twenty-four hours, yet some people are successful, while others are not. Some people are investing their time and energy on what they're passionate about, while others are wasting time in their comfort zone due to fear. Every day you wake up, you should be working on yourself and your dream. Every little thing matters. Success is the sum of all your efforts. So if you have to read a book on your craft or network at an event, do it. If you don't know what your dream is yet, have fun during the discovery. Worrying will not get you any closer to your dream. Try something new as much as you possibly can; you might discover your passion amid your curiosity. Do not stop until you find out what your dream is.

NO: There must be a bookstore in the afterlife if you've answered no. If so, I hope that there are Fruit by the Foots, Gushers, and Sandwiches Unlimited in heaven, too.

That was the last of the corresponding questions geared toward helping you figure out if your dream or whatever you're currently spending investing the majority of your time in is worth it. If you have answered *yes* more than you have answered *no*, then you have identified that what you're currently doing is worth it to you. If you have answered *no* more than you have answered *yes*, then you have identified that what you're currently doing is not worth it. With every question answered, I've left you tips and action steps that have worked for me; use them. My tips and strategies, or anyone else's, for that matter, won't work unless you apply them. Do not waste your time by simply reading this book and not applying any of its material. Knowledge is not power. The application of knowledge is power. When you are driving and you see a stop sign, you are supposed to stop. The sign itself means nothing if you don't apply your foot to the brake pedal and actually stop. If you don't stop, you run the risk of actually harming yourself or somebody else. The secrets of success won't work unless you take action.

There is no more room for indecisiveness. At this very moment in your life, you need to make a decision. For those who believe it is worth it, you've got to make the decision that you continue to work toward that dream, because it is the main reason blood is flowing through your veins right now. For those who are now aware that what you're doing is not worth the pain, you have to make the decision to find out what it is you're willing to pay the price for. This book was not meant to sugarcoat a thing. You can't possibly want the benefits of success without paying the costs. Fighting for your dream will cost you blood, sweat, tears, and a lot of money. However, once you've identified that it's worth it to you, it won't matter. Every setback will make you stronger and every failure will make you wiser.

I want to leave you with this: your story cannot be written without conflict. Something usually goes wrong before it goes right. Every movie has a plot twist, and every song has a bridge breaking up the repetitive pattern of a song that ultimately connects with the listener emotionally. Do not be intimidated by fear; embrace it. When you're scared to do something, that is a clear indication of what you should be doing. To me, fear is excitement turned inside out. You want to do it, but instead of running toward it, you run away from it. There's no other way to overcome a fear besides facing it. The ironic part is that most of us, including myself, have trouble facing our fears because we are our fears. We are scared of what we can actually accomplish. We are scared that what we actually want can actually happen. We are scared of being held accountable for such a grandiose task as living our life's purpose out loud. We are scared of this unfamiliar territory. I say to you, but also as a reminder to myself—don't be stingy with your gift. What you are meant to do during this lifetime, no one else can do. The lives you are meant to impact during this lifetime, no one else can impact. The legacy you are meant to leave during this lifetime, no one else can leave. Please do not block us from your blessings.

IS IT WORTH IT?
YES | NO

If your health is threatened, work. If disappointments surface, work. If your faith falters, work. If you inherit riches, continue to work. If your dreams are shattered and the star of hope begins to darken your horizon, work. If sorrow overwhelms you, or your friends prove untrue or desert you, work. If you are happy, keep right on working. No matter what ails you, work. Work as if your life depended on it, because it does.

— Dr. Dennis Kimbro

Consider it pure joy, my brothers, whenever you face trials of many kinds, because you know that the testing of your faith develops perseverance. Perseverance must finish its work so that you may be mature and complete, not lacking anything. If any of you lacks wisdom, he should ask God, who gives generously to all without finding fault, and it will be given to him. But when he asks, he must believe and not doubt, because he who doubts is like a wave of the sea, blown and tossed by the wind.

— James 1:2–9

WHAT ARE YOU WAITING FOR?

You're done reading this book,
And *you* deserve the *best* that life has to offer.
Pray often.
You woke up this morning,
While someone else is in a coffin.
Life is so short,
Yet we waste it for so long.
I hope that my words have lit a fire in your soul,
And you go find out *why* you were born!

Blessed is the man who perseveres under trial, because when he has stood the test, he will receive the crown of life that God has promised to those who love him.

— James 1:12

Made in the USA
Monee, IL
11 May 2021